The FINAL HELPING *of*

YOU MIGHT BE A REDNECK IF...

Jeff Foxworthy

Illustrations by David Boyd

LONGSTREET
Atlanta, Georgia

DEDICATION

To the three M's—
Maggie Houlehan, Mabel Segovia, and Mike Smardak—
who keep my life from being total chaos.
I never say thank you enough.

Published by
LONGSTREET, INC.
A subsidiary of Cox Newspapers
A subsidiary of Cox Enterprises, Inc.
2140 Newmarket Parkway
Suite 122
Marietta, GA 30067

Printed in the United States of America

1st printing 1999

Library of Congress Catalog Card Number: 99-60047
ISBN: 1-56352-575-5

Cover and book design by Burtch Hunter

FOREWORD

One of the questions I am asked most often is, "Did you ever, in your wildest dreams, imagine that the YOU MIGHT BE A REDNECK IF… jokes would be this big?" The answer, in a nutshell, is, "Nope."

The redneck jokes were born like most everything else I talk about on stage. I was just trying to find something I knew about that might make people laugh. I certainly knew about rednecks.

My definition of redneck, as I've explained many times, is "a glorious absence of sophistication." The condition is not affected by geography or annual income. Elvis made a lot of money, but everybody who has ever taken a tour of Graceland and reached the jungle room has thought, "Boy, you just can't give rednecks money." We love the songs, Elvis, but you should have left the carpet on the floor.

When I was growing up, my uncle painted the word *male* on the side of his mailbox as a joke. Unfortunately, I don't think many people got the joke. One day, while we were in high school, my cousin DeWayne pointed to the mailbox and said, "That ain't right…. That *m* is supposed to be capitalized." You could sense even then that DeWayne was destined for greatness.

Like most of my material, I have found that the closer I keep the redneck jokes to the truth, the better they work. For example, "…if you've ever used your ironing board for a buffet table" was inspired by my mother-in-law. She found it so effective that she continued to use it long after Thanksgiving was over.

"…if you have a complete set of salad bowls, and they all say Cool Whip on the side" is a tribute to my sister, who has yet to find a butter tub that she shouldn't save in the china cabinet.

One of my all-time favorites, "…if your working TV sits on top of your non-working TV" was apparently not exclusive to my grandparents. In fact, every time I tell it I notice a great deal of finger pointing in the audience.

While these jokes have always been a relatively short portion of my live show (perhaps five minutes out of two hours), they have become far more than simply a "bit." They became more than five million books and calendars. They became a huge reason for my selling more than ten million albums, including the No. 1 and No. 2 comedy albums of all time. They became T-shirts, hats, coffee mugs, and inter-office faxes. They became the reason people send me photos of their kids sledding on discarded car doors or manure spreaders covered in Christmas lights. They became the way people identified me – "Hey, it's the Redneck guy!"

I've been asked many times if I regret being know as "the Redneck guy, " but again the answer is, "Nope." I'm very grateful for all it has brought me and for the joy others have found in it. The fact that there are so many jokes has enabled me to constantly mix them up so I never get bored with them. What began as ten jokes scribbled on a yellow sheet of paper (since framed and hanging by our front door) has, through the years, become a list of a couple of thousand.

But there is no such thing as a bottomless pit. This horse has been ridden hard, so I thought before he killed over completely, why not lovingly put him out to pasture?

So it is with a little sadness that I declare this the last book of "You might be a redneck if…" jokes. Ever. This book will be the last in a series of great literary works that have proudly graced the backs of many a toilet across our great land. Thanks, Old Friend, for the wonderful ride. I now bid you adieu, never to be seen again…. Adios, amigos…. This is the final helping.

God Bless,

Jeff Foxworthy

P.S. If this book sells really well, or if I come up with other redneck lines I just can't keep to myself, then forget everything I just said.

God Bless You Again,

Jeff Foxworthy

YOU MIGHT BE A REDNECK IF...

You think a reservoir tip is
something they give you
on fishing shows.

Your shoelaces
used to be bailing wire.

The curtains in your living
room are camouflage.

You think four-on-the-floor
is a sleeping arrangement.

YOU MIGHT BE A REDNECK IF...

You've ever been paid in tomatoes.

YOU MIGHT BE A REDNECK IF...

The flowers in your bridal
bouquet were plastic.

Your bridal registry
is at Wal-Mart.

You valet park
at the dog track.

Your baby's first words
were "Rack 'em."

YOU MIGHT BE A REDNECK IF...

Your house has ever been
involved in a traffic accident.

YOU MIGHT BE A REDNECK IF...

It takes you longer than
two hours to check all of
your lottery tickets.

Your tablecloth was
delivered by the paper boy.

You wear your Marlboro
windbreaker to church.

You carry Ziploc bags in
your purse for leftovers.

YOU MIGHT BE A REDNECK IF...

You've ever mixed drinks
in an aquarium.

You've ever purchased
underwear and worn it
out of the store.

You hitch-hiked on vacation.

You bought a flea collar
for your possum.

YOU MIGHT BE A REDNECK IF...

You celebrate your bird-dog's birthday.

YOU MIGHT BE A REDNECK IF...

You wear cowboy boots
without socks.

Your best shoes used to be
someone else's.

Your biggest tax deduction
was bail money.

Your wife has ever won money
in a lumberjack competition.

YOU MIGHT BE A REDNECK IF...

You put beer on your cereal.

YOU MIGHT BE A REDNECK IF...

You can't remember where
your lawnmower is.

You have the deer cooler
on speed dial.

You have a turkey decoy
on layaway.

Your favorite recipe begins
with "Go possum hunting."

YOU MIGHT BE A REDNECK IF...

You love lard sandwiches.

YOU MIGHT BE A REDNECK IF...

Your idea of a night out is
chasing dogs through a swamp.

You fly fish with real flies.

You've ever spent more than
an hour in the grocery store
looking for Venison Helper.

Your dream home
is a bass boat.

YOU MIGHT BE A REDNECK IF...

Your coffee table
is also a cooler.

The phone number for a
pizza delivery company is
written on the wall
above your phone.

There are more clothes on
your floor than in
your drawers.

You're listed as "uninsurable"
and you're not yet out
of high school.

YOU MIGHT BE A REDNECK IF...

There are hoof prints
on your carpet.

YOU MIGHT BE A REDNECK IF...

You were wearing a John Deere
hat in your senior picture.

You've ever bought a round
of pickled pigs feet.

Your security system is
a latch on your screen door.

You turn the sprinkler on
and tell your kids it's
a water park.

YOU MIGHT BE A REDNECK IF...

People can tell what
you had for breakfast
by looking in your beard.

YOU MIGHT BE A REDNECK IF...

Your favorite restaurant
has a sawdust floor.

Your favorite recipe
includes Vienna Sausage.

You're saving up to
"gravel" your driveway.

The fireworks stand
gives you a volume discount.

YOU MIGHT BE A REDNECK IF...

You ever got into a fight
over an inner tube.

YOU MIGHT BE A REDNECK IF...

Your trash collector isn't
sure about what stays
and what goes.

The deer head over
your fireplace is wearing
your Mardi Gras beads.

You've ever had a dream
about beef jerky.

Your dog buries bones
in the middle of your
living room.

YOU MIGHT BE A REDNECK IF...

You've ever
made love in a car . . .
that was being towed.

You take a sidearm
with you to the mailbox.

Your work bench used
to be your front door.

You missed sex education
class because your
baby was sick.

YOU MIGHT BE A REDNECK IF...

YOU MIGHT BE A REDNECK IF...

Your carpool has its
own fight song.

You've ever used Pam
for shoe polish.

You've ever made a flower
box out of a concrete block.

You've sent fan mail
to a monster truck.

YOU MIGHT BE A REDNECK IF...

The sheriff regularly speaks to you through a megaphone.

YOU MIGHT BE A REDNECK IF...

You have a family portrait
by a courtroom artist.

You remember where you
were when J.R. was shot.

It's impossible to reach your
trailer without getting
your feet wet.

Your wife wears chip clips
in her hair.

YOU MIGHT BE A REDNECK IF...

The best photo of you has a height chart as a backdrop.

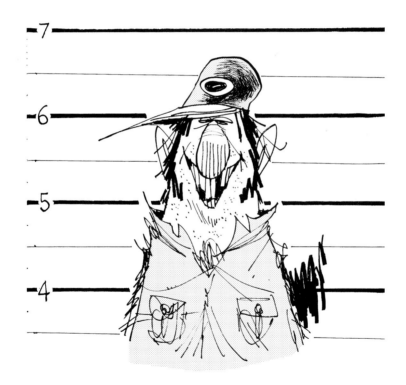

YOU MIGHT BE A REDNECK IF...

All you get on your TV
is the sound.

You put Alka-Seltzer in
cheap wine to get
"champagne."

You think common stock is a
pig owned by more than
one person.

You try to make at least one
crank call a day.

YOU MIGHT BE A REDNECK IF...

You regard deer processing
as an art form.

You've received a lifetime
achievement award from
a liquor store.

You've ever practiced
someone else's signature.

You've used food stamps
on a date.

YOU MIGHT BE A REDNECK IF...

There were dogs in the church
on your wedding day.

YOU MIGHT BE A REDNECK IF...

Your spring cleaning consists
of detonating bug bombs.

Your wife still wears a
mini-skirt eight months
into pregnancy.

You've lived in three different
homes at the same address.

You make your own soap
in the same pot you
make jelly in.

YOU MIGHT BE A REDNECK IF...

You can see your bottom lip
without a mirror.

YOU MIGHT BE A REDNECK IF...

You list "staring"
amongst your hobbies.

Property downwind of your
home is virtually worthless.

You mouth the lines
while watching
"Dukes of Hazzard" reruns.

You were the inspiration
for prescription-strength
Bean-O.

YOU MIGHT BE A REDNECK IF...

You've ever had to shoot the lock off your own front door.

YOU MIGHT BE A REDNECK IF...

The only time you moved
was under a witness
protection program.

The only blood test
you ever had was at
a police station.

The local tattoo parlor
runs specials on your
sister's name.

The FBI has more pictures
of your family than you do.

YOU MIGHT BE A REDNECK IF...

You steal the towels when
you stay overnight
with relatives.

Your tools are worth
more than your car.

You removed the bathroom
door so you could watch
TV from the commode.

You carry pictures of your
coon dogs in your wallet.

YOU MIGHT BE A REDNECK IF...

You wear
a baseball cap to bed.

YOU MIGHT BE A REDNECK IF...

Your decision to start a family
was made at a truck stop.

You bought your
wedding dress at a yard sale.

Your wife bought Caller ID
so she'd know which bar
you're in.

Your daughter's bridal
registry is at Ace Hardware.

YOU MIGHT BE A REDNECK IF...

Any of your children were
conceived at a traffic signal.

YOU MIGHT BE A REDNECK IF...

Your favorite T-shirt has
started more than one fight.

You like to take your own
mattress along on a trip.

Your brothers convinced you
that you were an only child.

You've ever used a tablespoon
as a shoe horn.

YOU MIGHT BE A REDNECK IF...

You've broken a speed limit
in reverse.

YOU MIGHT BE A REDNECK IF...

You had your anniversary
dinner at the food court
in the mall.

You've ever hitch-hiked
to the liquor store.

Your home security system
is a "Bad Dog" sign.

You think an optimist
is an eye doctor.

YOU MIGHT BE A REDNECK IF...

You hand-painted the
white walls on
your tires yourself.

Your wedding band turned
green on your honeymoon.

The slip cover on your sofa
used to be a shower curtain.

You broke a toe when
you dropped your
belt buckle on it.

YOU MIGHT BE A REDNECK IF...

You've given mouth-to-mouth
resuscitation to a dog.

YOU MIGHT BE A REDNECK IF...

You're driving the car
being described by
the police scanner.

Your dog's so mean
you have to pick up your
mail in town.

You don't have electricity
in every room in your house.

The last time you
test drove a car it ended
in a police chase.

YOU MIGHT BE A REDNECK IF...

You have a framed portrait
of a hog.

YOU MIGHT BE A REDNECK IF...

You've had more wives
than jobs.

Your doorbell plays
"Freebird."

You enjoy full cable service
when your neighbor leaves
his curtains open.

You learned to drive
by watching
"Smokey and the Bandit."

YOU MIGHT BE A REDNECK IF...

You're smoking in
your driver's license photo.

YOU MIGHT BE A REDNECK IF...

Your doctor prescribes
moonshine as a painkiller.

You proposed to your wife
through a mouthful of Cheetos.

Your honeymoon began
in a Motel 6 and ended
in a holding cell.

You've ever asked for
layaway at a yard sale.

YOU MIGHT BE A REDNECK IF...

You ever had sex
in a tornado shelter.

An episode of
"Walker, Texas Ranger"
changed your life.

You're on a salvage yard's
mailing list.

Your wedding cake
was made by Sara Lee.

YOU MIGHT BE A REDNECK IF...

You've unstopped a sink with a shotgun.

YOU MIGHT BE A REDNECK IF...

Your birthstone
is cubic zirconia.

Kissing your cousin goodbye
is a five-minute job.

Your dog was neutered
by court order.

Your family reunions resemble
the "Jerry Springer Show."

YOU MIGHT BE A REDNECK IF...

The doctor
who delivers your children
also delivers your propane.

YOU MIGHT BE A REDNECK IF...

You work on your car
when there's nothing
wrong with it.

You've never bought a car
you could drive home.

You treat your arthritis
with WD40.

Your favorite poem
is from a restroom wall.

YOU MIGHT BE A REDNECK IF...

You ever gift-wrapped a tire.

YOU MIGHT BE A REDNECK IF...

You practice skeet shooting
with hubcaps.

Your sister wrote off
her boob job as a
"business expense."

You've exceeded 90 mph
in a bass boat.

You have visitation rights
to a dog.

YOU MIGHT BE A REDNECK IF...

Your honeymoon
hotel advertised
"Truckers welcome."

Your wedding shirt
had cut-off sleeves.

Your wife's work number
begins with 1-900.

Your prom featured
a wet T-shirt contest.

YOU MIGHT BE A REDNECK IF...

Your dentures
have fillings.

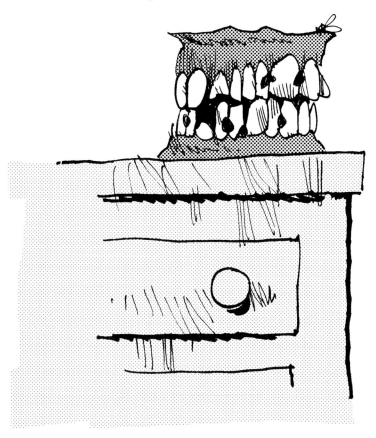

YOU MIGHT BE A REDNECK IF...

Your best watch came free
with ten gallons of gas.

Every car you own
is permanently for sale.

You send fan mail
to the Shopping Channel.

Sex education at your school
included advice on avoiding
the steering wheel.

YOU MIGHT BE A REDNECK IF...

The collar on your dog
costs more than what you
are wearing.

YOU MIGHT BE A REDNECK IF...

Your Christmas tree came
from an interstate median.

Your basketball hoop
was a fishing net.

A judge sentences you
to "the usual."

You make your only phone
call from jail to a
1-900 number.

YOU MIGHT BE A REDNECK IF...

Your kids take roadkill
to show and tell.

YOU MIGHT BE A REDNECK IF...

Tying your shoelaces
gives you a headache.

Your wedding vows consist
of "same as last time."

Your wife's nail polish
is auto touch-up paint.

Your family car has flames
painted down both sides.

YOU MIGHT BE A REDNECK IF...

The last thing your ex-wife
said to you was,
"It's me or them dogs."

You make your own beef jerky.

Your kids' grades dropped
when you started helping
with their homework.

Your "business number"
is a bar's pay phone.

YOU MIGHT BE A REDNECK IF...

You ever surrendered to the
police in exchange
for cigarettes.

YOU MIGHT BE A REDNECK IF...

Your Fourth of July fireworks
are distress flares.

You call the church
where you were married
"the scene of the crime."

You've head-butted
a vending machine.

You want
"Achy Breaky Heart"
played at your funeral.

YOU MIGHT BE A REDNECK IF...

There's a pair of
needle nose pliers
in your medicine cabinet.

YOU MIGHT BE A REDNECK IF...

You've ever mooned a jury.

You get the wholesale price
on pregnancy test kits.

Your wife went into labor
during your wedding ceremony.

At least one dog slept in your
bed on your wedding night.

YOU MIGHT BE A REDNECK IF...

Any of your sisters
work in construction.

YOU MIGHT BE A REDNECK IF...

In preparation for a romantic
evening, you stop by the
grocery store for a bottle
of Mr. Bubble.

Winn-Dixie catered
your wedding.

You use White-Out
to do a French manicure.

Your wife considers
a pizza with all the works
"gourmet dining."

YOU MIGHT BE A REDNECK IF...

The miniature figures
atop your wedding cake
were wearing overalls.

You're seen smoking on the
church Christmas parade float.

Your pawn shop
sends you a Christmas card.

You ever videotaped
a yard sale.

YOU MIGHT BE A REDNECK IF...

You need pliers to change
the channels on your TV.

YOU MIGHT BE A REDNECK IF...

You have separate mortgages
for your home and
the land it's parked on.

You've held a business lunch
at a vending machine.

All the major fast-food chains
are represented on the floor
of your car.

Your hope chest
is a Styrofoam cooler.

YOU MIGHT BE A REDNECK IF...

You ever waved at traffic from your front porch wearing just your underwear.

YOU MIGHT BE A REDNECK IF...

You think NASA
is an auto parts store.

You've worn your
Waffle House uniform
on a date.

One hole in the ozone layer
has been traced to your car.

You think a 401(k) is
your mother-in-law's bra size.

YOU MIGHT BE A REDNECK IF...

The local funeral parlor has a happy hour before every burial.

YOU MIGHT BE A REDNECK IF...

Your resume includes your
high scores on video games.

You're using udder cream
as moisturizer.

You've sold a car
to settle a bar tab.

All your home electronics
have the serial numbers
filed off.

YOU MIGHT BE A REDNECK IF...

You've been hospitalized
after a chili cook-off.

Picking out a burial plot
involved wandering around
your yard.

You had to schedule your
honeymoon around
school vacations.

You've driven for over a month
on a baby spare tire.

YOU MIGHT BE A REDNECK IF...

All you see in your rearview mirror are dogs.

YOU MIGHT BE A REDNECK IF...

You've ever hunted within spitting distance of your front porch.

You run out to get the morning newspaper wearing nothing but a smile.

Your kid takes jumper cables to show and tell.

Your RV is bigger than your house.

YOU MIGHT BE A REDNECK IF...

You get a clear picture only
when your cat sits on the TV.

YOU MIGHT BE A REDNECK IF...

You honeymooned
in the camper shell
of your pick-up truck.

Your daughter's Barbie Dream
House has a clothesline
in the front yard.

Your favorite Mexican food
is Doritos.

A tree falls through your roof
and you decide to leave it.

YOU MIGHT BE A REDNECK IF...

You're still keeping a goldfish
in the plastic bag you won it in.

YOU MIGHT BE A REDNECK IF...

You can't remember
what the blue tarp in your
front yard is covering.

You've repaired a broken vase
with Polygrip.

Nobody in your
family dances . . . for free.

Your toupee
was made by your taxidermist.

YOU MIGHT BE A REDNECK IF...

Your grandmother has been
busted more than once
in a bingo raid.

You can open a beer
one-handed.

Kids knock on your door
as a dare.

All you can see in your
rearview mirror is smoke.

YOU MIGHT BE A REDNECK IF...

You ever belched
the words
"not guilty."

YOU MIGHT BE A REDNECK IF...

The most romantic moment
of your life was captured
on a security camera.

You bought your wife's
birthday present at
the Gun & Tackle Shop.

The longest conversation
you've had all week
was with a turkey.

Your wife is turned on by the
sound of a trolling motor.

YOU MIGHT BE A REDNECK IF...

Your guard dog is kept chained
to a propane tank.

YOU MIGHT BE A REDNECK IF...

People see things on your
clothesline that causes them
to lose sleep.

You own camouflage
toilet paper.

Your wife stores onions in
pantyhose in the living room.

You fixed your clogged septic
tank with a little dynamite.

YOU MIGHT BE A REDNECK IF...

You ever used duct tape
to seal your casserole
for the church supper.

YOU MIGHT BE A REDNECK IF...

You ever used your air
compressor to clean up
after a party.

The judge tells you that
shooting crows is not
a community service.

You leave your dogs
to babysit the kids.

You can forecast the weather
by looking at "woolly worms."

YOU MIGHT BE A REDNECK IF...

You named each of
your kids after the car they
were conceived in.

YOU MIGHT BE A REDNECK IF...

Your co-workers start
a petition for you
to change your socks.

Your idea of
a drive-by shooting involves
a shotgun and a stop sign.

You've ever been tracked
by bloodhounds.

Your daddy married
your old girlfriend.